This book is dedicated to all the wild animals that have blessed me with beautiful windows into their lives.

Baby Animals
Moving

SUZI ESZTERHAS

Owlkids Books

Animals spend a lot of their time on the move, looking for food, water, and safe places to rest. Some baby animals are born ready to walk, climb, or swim. Others need help getting from place to place. Let's follow these baby animals and see how they get around!

A zebra calf can stand up just minutes after it's born. Within a few hours, this foal can walk, gallop, and run with his herd. Off we go!

This baby orangutan hangs on to his mother as she swings through the jungle. Soon he will swing from tree to tree on his own. Wheee!

Splish, splash! A black-necked stilt chick walks in the sand. It won't be long before she learns to fly.

This egret chick wants to fly but he doesn't have all of his feathers yet. He practices flapping his wings anyway. One day he will soar through the skies!

A warthog piglet runs through the grass with her brother. The siblings stick together and move fast to stay safe from predators. Quick, quick, little piggies!

Before it learns to swim, a sea otter pup rides on Mom's belly to stay warm and dry. What a cozy way to travel!

These lion cubs are out for a family walk. When a cub gets tired, mother lion carries him in her mouth. She is careful not to hurt him with her teeth.

This kangaroo joey can't hop very far, so he travels in his mother's pouch. In a few weeks, he will hop along on his own.

Hold on tight! A cute koala hitches a ride on Mom's back. By the time she turns one she will climb trees all by herself.

An elephant calf must travel to get water every day. His mother shows the way by gently nudging him with her trunk.

As the herd parades through the field it stays close together to protect the calf from predators.

It's a hot day and Mom wants to cool off, but these young bear cubs are scared of the water. A piggyback ride makes them feel safe.

Orca calves are strong swimmers. They dive and flip as they move through the ocean with their family pod. Sometimes they swim for miles to find fish to eat. See you later, orcas!

Suzi Eszterhas

Sloths only come down from the trees about once a week (to poop!). I had to climb high up a tree in the rain forest of Costa Rica to snap a photo of this sleepy baby and its mom.

Hi, I'm Suzi!

I travel all over the world taking pictures of animals. I also help animal conservationists by telling their stories and helping raise money for their causes. When I'm not snapping photos, I like talking to people about how they can help wild animals. I think it's important for kids to connect with animals and nature. You can do this by looking at photos, reading books, or just going outside and running, climbing, and jumping like these baby animals on the move!

Baby animals spend a lot of time watching their parents and copying their behavior. During a family walk, these polar bear cubs took their steps at exactly the same time as Mom.

Lemur babies are born with a strong grip. This baby was holding on tight as I took a photo.

Mountain gorillas usually move slowly and stop to rest often. This baby found a comfy spot for the long jungle walk!

This tigress was taking her cubs on their first forest walk. They had never been away from their den before! I spent months taking photos of this family, watching the cubs grow, play, sleep, and explore.

As a wildlife photographer, I have to follow animals while they are moving. Sometimes I keep up with them on foot, but other times I follow them in boats, planes, or safari jeeps like this one!

Baby rhinos always stick close to their moms. I followed behind this duo as they wandered through the fields munching on grass.

Consultant: Chris Earley, Interpretive Biologist, University of Guelph Arboretum

Owlkids Books acknowledges the financial support of the Canada Council for the Arts, the Ontario Arts Council, the Government of Canada through the Canada Book Fund (CBF) and the Government of Ontario through the Ontario Media Development Corporation's Book Initiative for our publishing activities.

Published in Canada by
Owlkids Books Inc.
10 Lower Spadina Avenue
Toronto, ON M5V 2Z2

Published in the United States by
Owlkids Books Inc.
1700 Fourth Street
Berkeley, CA 94710

Library and Archives Canada Cataloguing in Publication

Eszterhas, Suzi, author, photographer
　　Baby animals moving / written and photographed by Suzi Eszterhas.

(Baby animals)
ISBN 978-1-77147-299-9 (hardcover)

　　1. Animal locomotion--Juvenile literature. 2. Animal behavior-- Juvenile literature.
3. Animals--Infancy--Pictorial works--Juvenile literature. I. Title.

QP301.E89 2018　　　　　j591.5'7　　　　　C2017-903873-7

Library of Congress Control Number: 2017943548

Edited by: Jackie Farquhar
Designed by: Danielle Arbour

Manufactured in Dongguan, China, in September 2017, by Toppan Leefung Packaging & Printing (Dongguan) Co., Ltd.
Job #BAYDC44

A　　　B　　　C　　　D　　　E　　　F

Publisher of Chirp, chickaDEE and OWL
www.owlkidsbooks.com

Owlkids Books is a division of